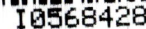

I0568428

Bread in a good way
© Piffz, 2016
www.piffz.com

1. edition, 1. printing
Printed in EU 2016

ISBN 978-87-93084-26-1

© 2016 Author: Patricia Olivia Stewer

Cover and graphic design:
Yummp Design Studio - www.yummp.net

 PIFFZ

Bread in a good way

by Patricia Olivia Stewer

PIFFZ

www.piffz.com

Index

Intro   7

SugarBuns   10

26 Hours Ciabatta Loaves   14

Bagels   18

Foccacia Bread   22

White Bread   26

Carrot Buns   30

Italian Buns   34

Muesli Buns   38

Naan Bread   42

Vanilla Buns   46

Intro

There is nothing in the world so wonderful as to bake. Feel the doughs soft structure between your fingers and feel how a bowl full of ingredients can be assembled and become a wonderful dough that ends up filling the home with a warm, intense scent of fresh bread.

In this book, I have collected 10 of my favorite recipes for bread and buns. Actually it's the 10 that I use every week to feed my family.

Every morning I either bake vanilla buns, muesli buns or Italian buns and often comes neighbors or good friends to a cup of morning coffee and a bun when the kids are sent to school. I believe that homemade bread is the best for my children. That way I know that what they eat is fresh.

Good luck and bon appétit.

Sugar Buns

Approx. 16 buns

Warm the milk and dissolve the yeast in it. Add the melted butter.

Add salt, sugar and egg and mix then the flour.

INGREDIENTS

250 g milk

25 g yeast

100 g butter

1 egg

1/2 tsp salt

100 g sugar

$ tsp cardamon

600 g flour

Knead the dough well together until the dough releases the fingers and let it rise in a bowl for 40 minutes covered by a damp tea towel ..

Molds and let them rise for 30 minutes.

Brush with water and sprinkle them with sugar.

Bake for 10 minutes at 250 ° C in the middle of the oven.

26 Hours Ciabatta Loaves

Approx. 3 Flutes or 8 Buns

DAY 1

Dissolve yeast in water and mix the flour in. Stir it well together into a smooth paste.

DAY 2

Dissolve yeast in water. Use dough from day 1. Pour it into the mixer along with salt and flour. Mix it in the mixer for 15 minutes until the dough is "long".

Grease a large baking pan with oil. Spread dough in the pan and let it rise covered for 1 hour.

Divide the dough into 3 pieces. Place them on a plate and sprinkle a little flour over and let them rise another 30 minutes. You could try to Twist the ends slightly.

Turn oven to 250 ° C. Set the the buns in the oven and bake for 5 minutes. Set the heat down to 200 ° C and spray water on the buns with a water atomizer. Bake for 10 minutes additional.

Spray water on the buns and bake them for the last time for 10 minutes.

When they're done, take them out and spray them with water again.

It is best if you remove them from the plate, otherwise they become soft at the bottom. Place them on a rack or in a bread basket.

INGREDIENTS

DAY 1

250 g fingerwarm water

5 g yeast

250 g flour

DAY 2

10 g yeast

4 tsp salt

250 g fingerwarm water

450 - 500 g flour

Olive Oil

Bagels

Approx. 12 Bagels

Add yeast, sugar, and salt to the water.
Add the flour a little at a time.
Run the mixer for 5-10 minutes until the dough seems compact and "long".
Let the dough rise covered for 1 hour.
Knead the dough on a table and divide it into 12 pieces. Form into buns and make a hole in each bun.
Put them to rise for 30 minutes.

Turn oven to 175 ° C. Put water into a medium saucepan. Add a little salt.
Boil 2 bagels at a time so they have room. They must be boiled 3 minutes on each side.
Place them to dry on a tea towel.
Put them on a baking sheet and brush with egg white. Perhaps sprinkle with garnish or flavor (For example: Sesame seeds, chili powder or grated cheese).

Bake in center of oven for 15-20 minutes.

TIP:
You can also mix something into the dough, for example. sundried tomatoes, oregano. It gives them a good taste for dinner. Or for breakfast with vanilla or cinnamon.

INGREDIENTS

25 g yeast

500 g fingerwarm water

3 tbsp sugar

2 tsp salt

850 g flour

Phbs. poppy seeds, sesame, chili powder, or something else to spice the bagel.

Foccacia Bread

Approx. 12 Bagels

INGREDIENTS

2 tbsp olive oil

540 g flour

2 tsb kosher salt

25 g yeast

400 g fungerwarm water

TOPPING

Olive oil

3-4 cloves of garlic

2 tbsp fresh herbs, ex. rosemary, thyme, and oregano, or 1 tsp dry herbs

1-2 tbsp salt

Grated cheese

PREPARATION

Mix everything together in a bowl and let rise for an hour, covered and warm, or in a plastic bowl with lid in hot water to the lid pops ..

Mix the garlic in olive oil ... Put the dough in a paper-clad roasting pan. Spread dough with a spatula with oil. Make small holes in the dough and spread the garlic oil in them.

Sprinkle with salt and cheese and optionally herbs.

You can also decorate with feta and black olives and small sliced tomatoes or just what you want.

Baking time: Approx 25 min. at 225 ° C.

White Bread

1 Bread

Dissolve yeast in water.
Add the oil, salt, sugar and half of the flour. Add remaining flour a little at a time, allowing you constantly to have control over the dough .
Let your mixer work for you until the dough is kneaded thoroughly.

Let dough rise covered in a mixing bowl for approx. 45 minutes to double the size.

Knead again the dough through the machine, and continue on the table.
Divide the dough in two and put them in separate tins. Cover and let them rise for 45 minutes until doubled in size.

Place the loaves in a 200 ° C oven on a rack in the lower groove in 15 minutes. After that you move the rack one notch up and bake for another 15 minutes.

When the loaves are done, brush with a little water. Let them cool on a wire rack.

INGREDIENTS

600 g water

25 g yeast

2 tbspoil

1 tsp salt

1tbsp sugar

approx. 900 g flour

Carrot
Buns

Approx. 16 Buns

250 g carrots

15 g yeast

250 g water

250 g natural yogurt

150 g oat meal

Approx. 450 g flour

1 1/2 tsp salt

PREPARATION

Peel and grate the carrots finely. Stir the yeast into finger warm water and add yogurt, oatmeal, carrots and salt. Add the flour a little at a time and knead dough thoroughly. Allow to rise covered until doubled in size - approx. 1 hour.

Put the dough on the table and shape into approx. 16 buns and place them on a baking sheet . Hereafter rise covered for 30-45 minutes.

Brush with water and sprinkle with oatmeal. Bake the rolls approx. 20 minutes at 200 ° C in the middle of the oven. Cool on wire rack.

Italian Buns

Approx. 12 Buns

Mix all ingredients together in the mixer. Let it knead for 10 minutes until the dough becomes long.

Rise at room temperature approx. 4 hours or in the refrigerator overnight.

Bake for approx. 20 minutes at 250 ° C

TIP:
In order to form the molds, dip your hands in cold water - that will help the dough not to stick to your hands.

INGREDIENTS

500 g water

25 g yeast

2 tsp salt

3 tbsp oil

88 g flour

Muesli Buns

Approx. 16 Buns

40 g water

50 g yeast

300 g milk

50 g butter

Approx. 450 g flour

1 tsp salt

3 tbsp sugar

1 tsp cardamon

100 g muesli

PREPARATION

Dissolve the yeast in the finger warm water. Add the remaining ingredients and knead dough together.

Form 16 buns and place them on a plate. Turn oven to 200 ° C and leave the rolls under a damp towel for 25-30 minutes.

Bake for approx. 9 minutes in the middle of the oven.

LANDHAUS KOERBCHEN

Naan Bread

Approx. 6 Bread

INGREDIENTS

250 g mailk

2 eggs

2 tsp sugar

1 tsp baking powder

1/2 tsp soda

1 pinch salt

600 - 650 g flour

Nigella seeds

PREPARATION

Mix all the dry ingredients in a bowl and mix milk and egg in another.
Add the contents of both bowls in a mixer and knead the dough till it is smooth. Knead it on the table.

Divide the dough into 6 buns and roll them with a rolling pin until they are about the size of your pan.

Put some butter and oil in the pan and bake the bread in the pan approx. 4 minutes on each side over low heat.

Sprinkle with nigella seeds.

Vanilla Buns

Approx. 16 Buns

40 g water

50 g yeast

300 g milk

50 g butter

Approx. 450 g flour

1 tsp salt

3 tbsp sugar

2 tsp vanilla

PREPARATION

Dissolve the yeast in the finger warm water. Add the remaining ingredients and knead dough together.

Form 16 buns and place them on a plate. Turn oven to 200 ° C and leave the rolls under a damp towel for 25-30 minutes.

Bake for approx. 9 minutes in the middle of the oven.